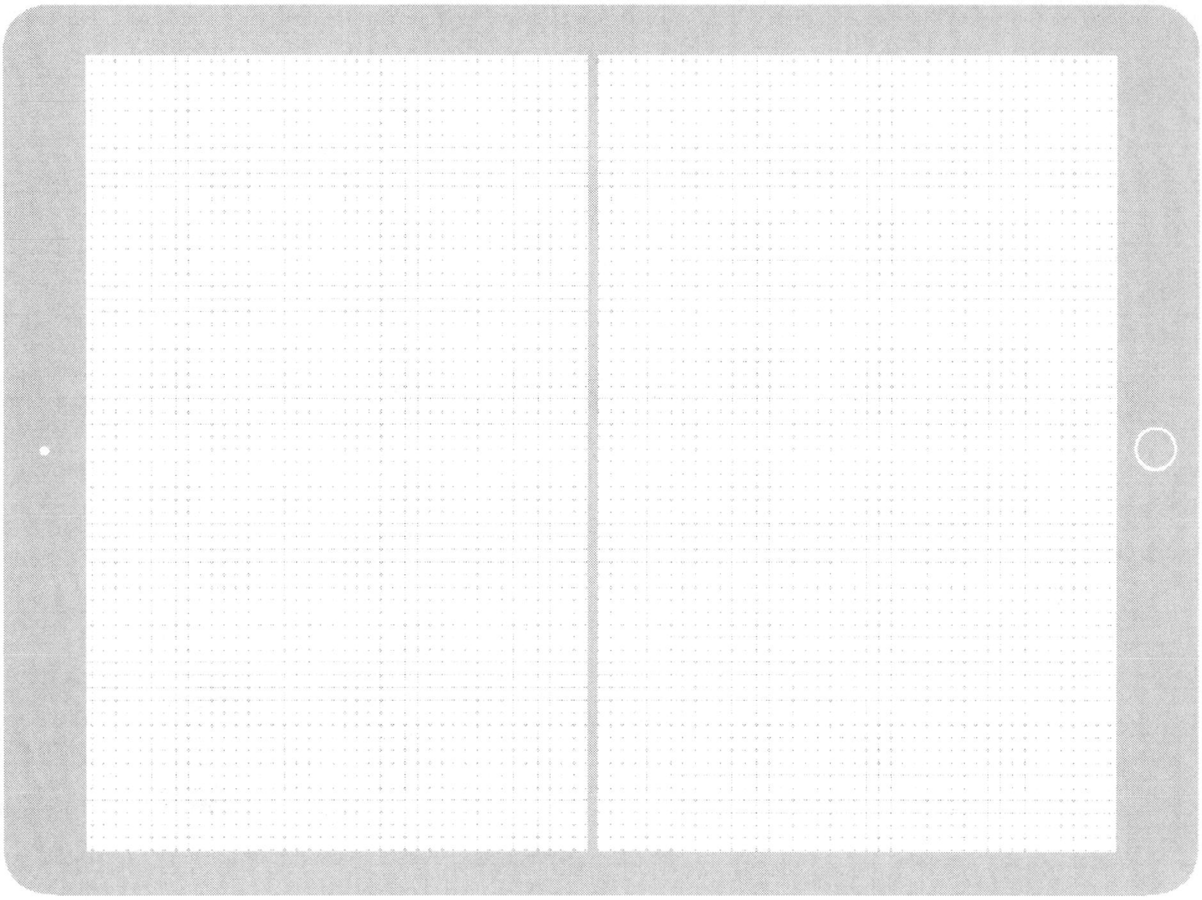

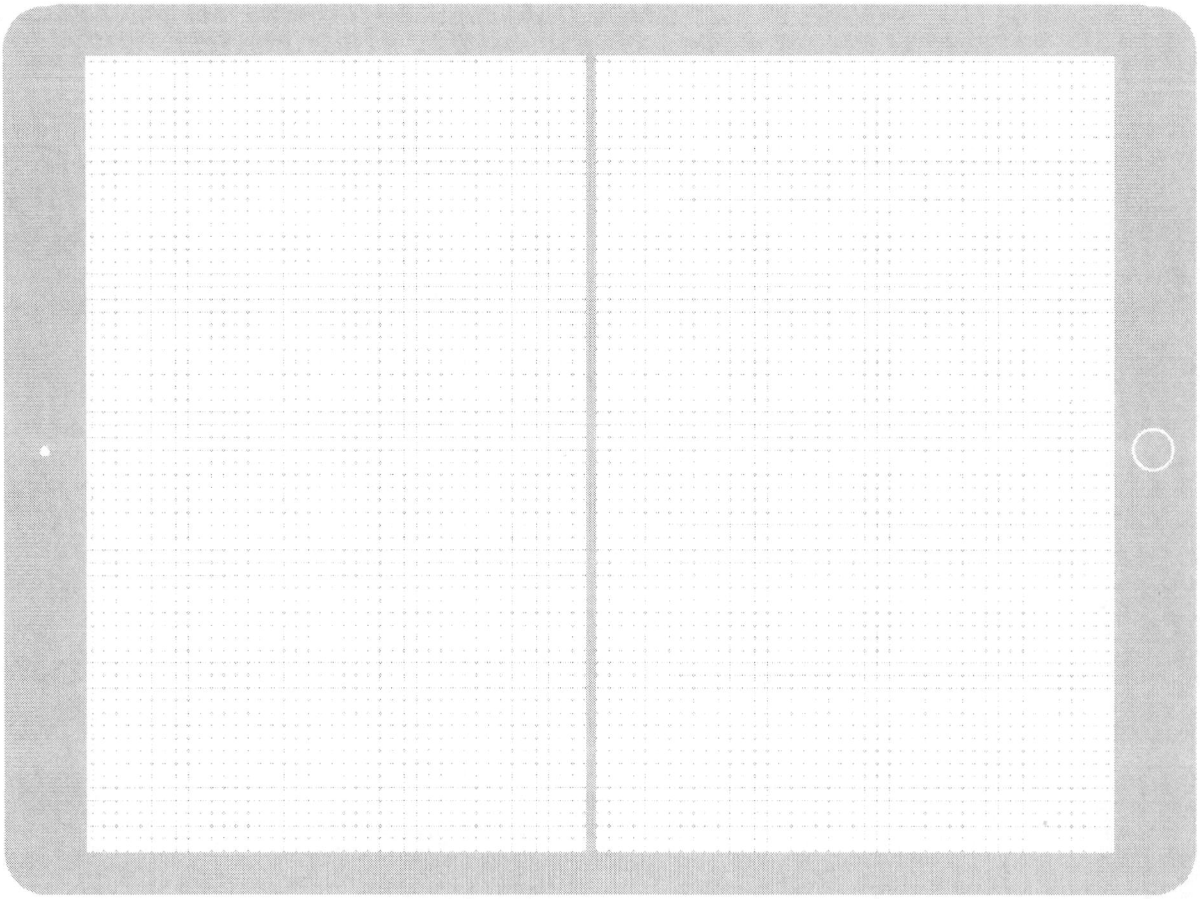

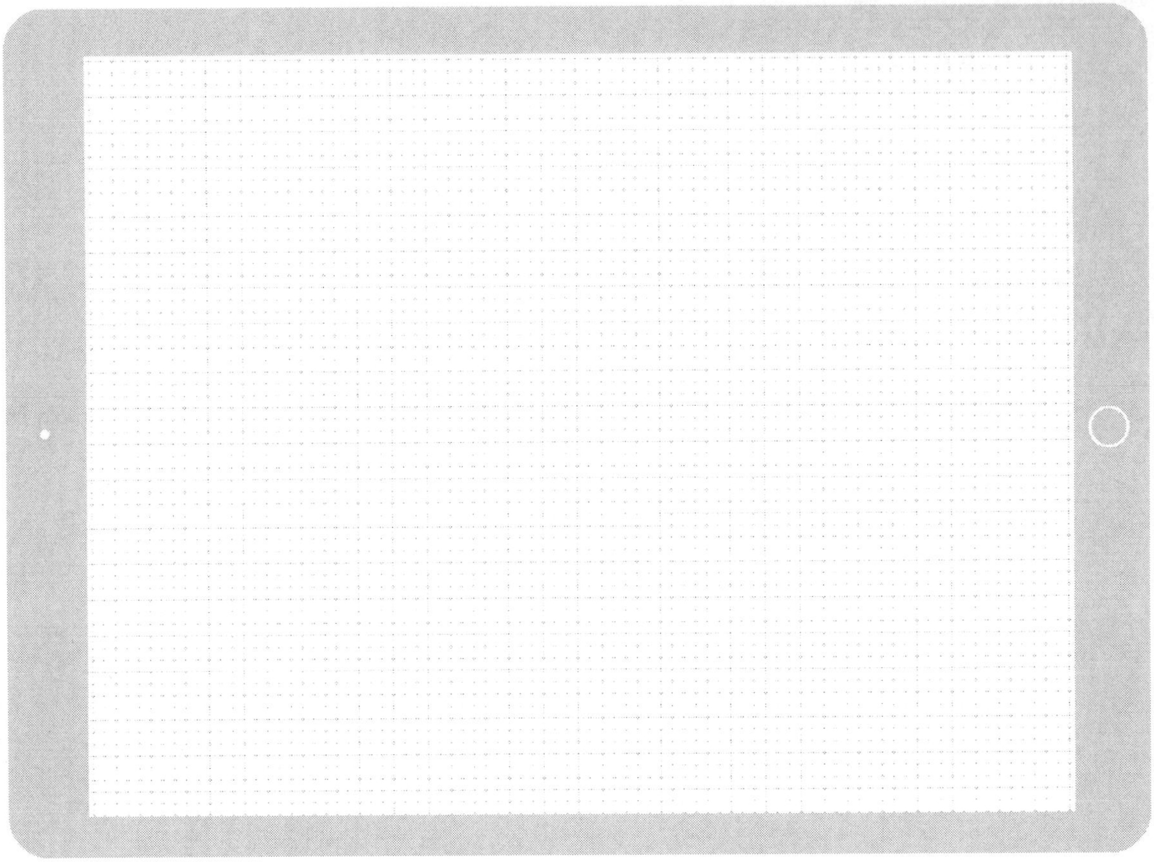

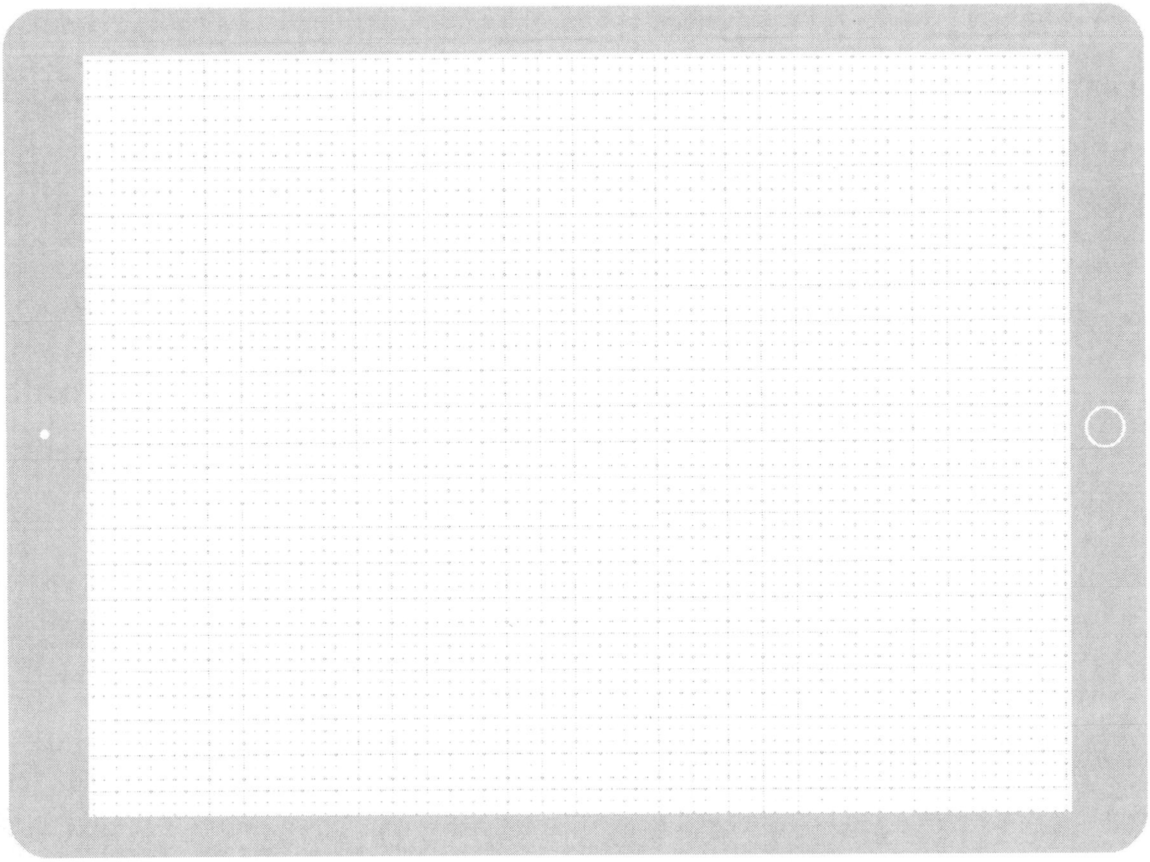

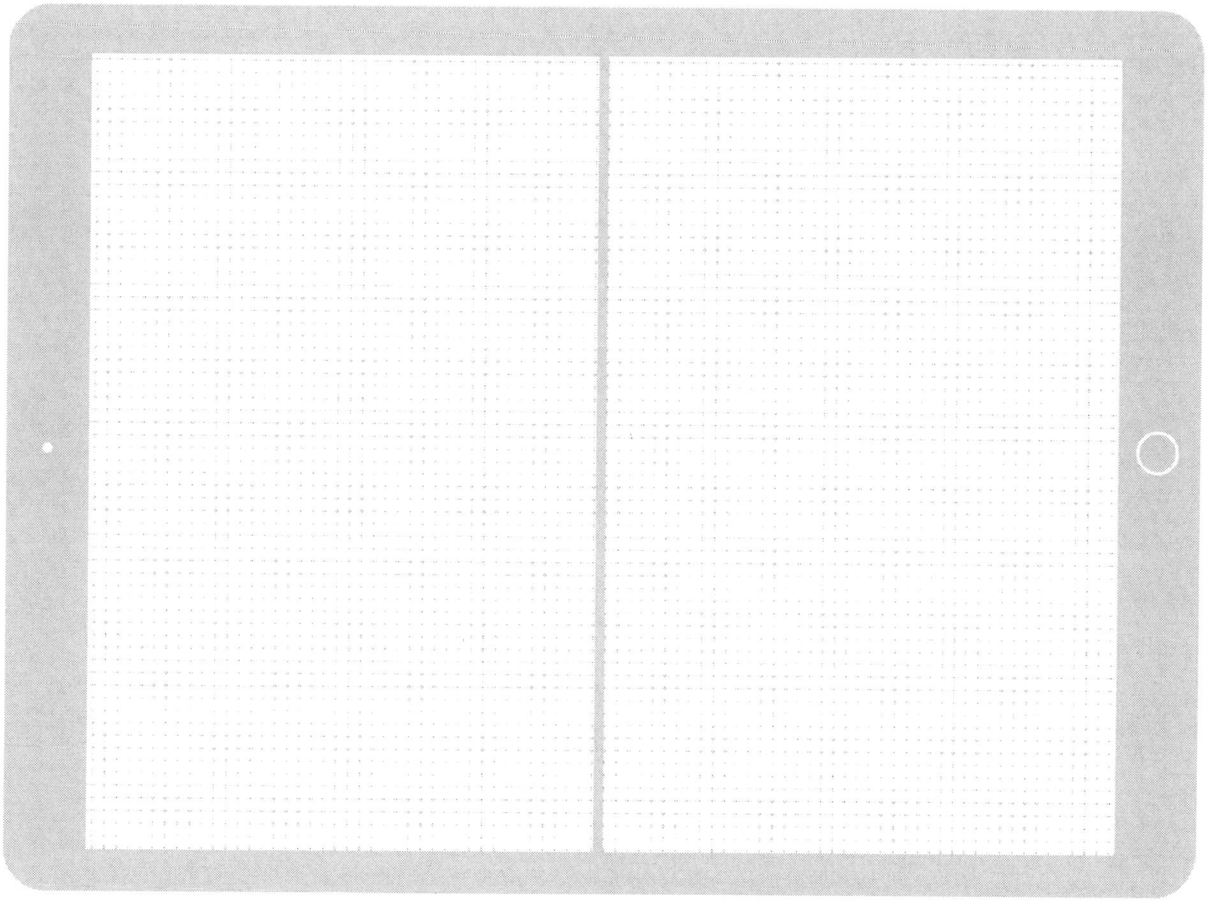

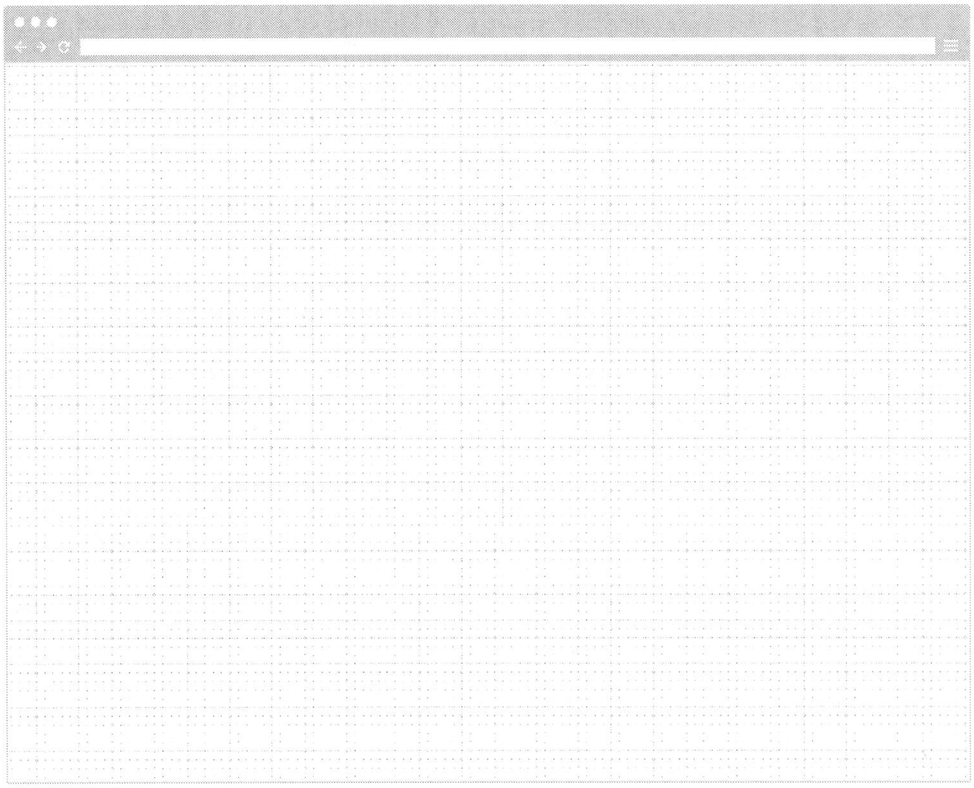

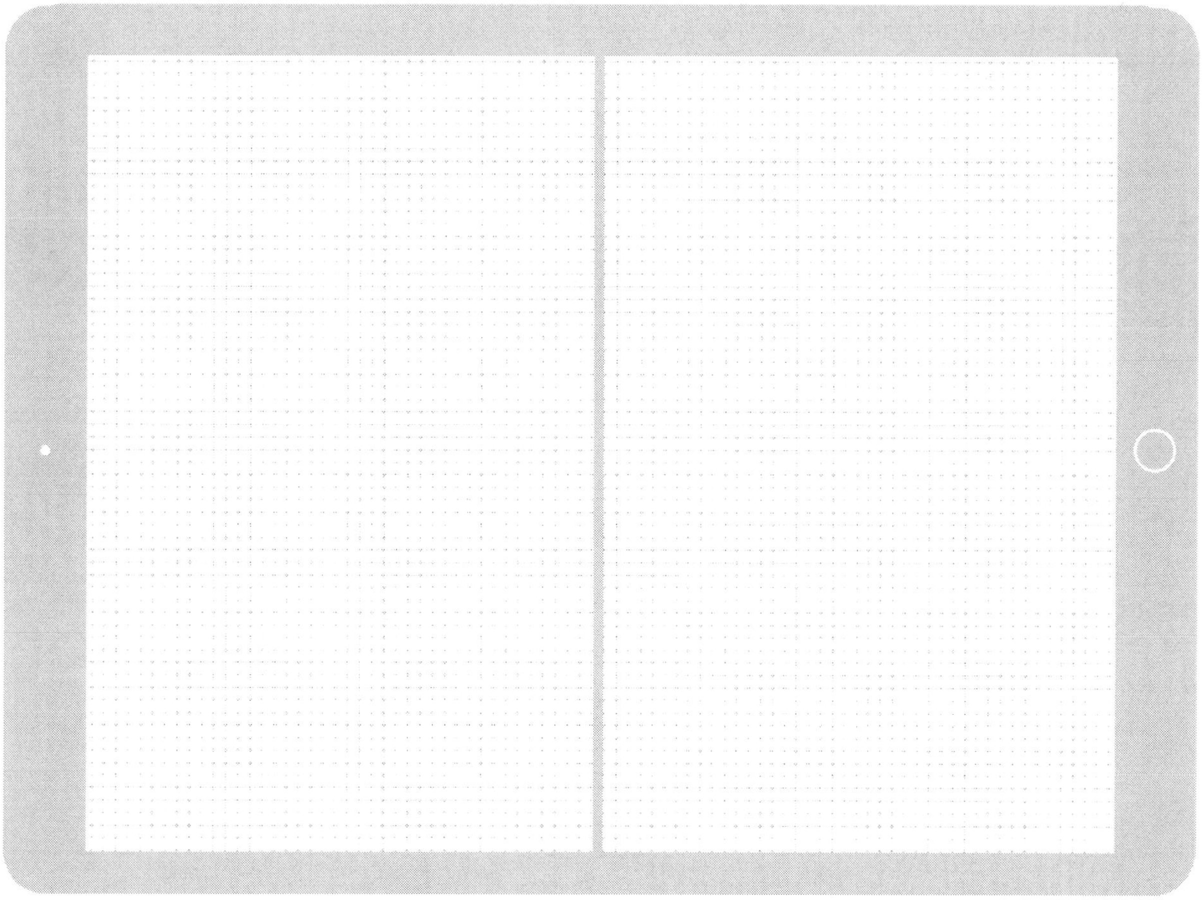

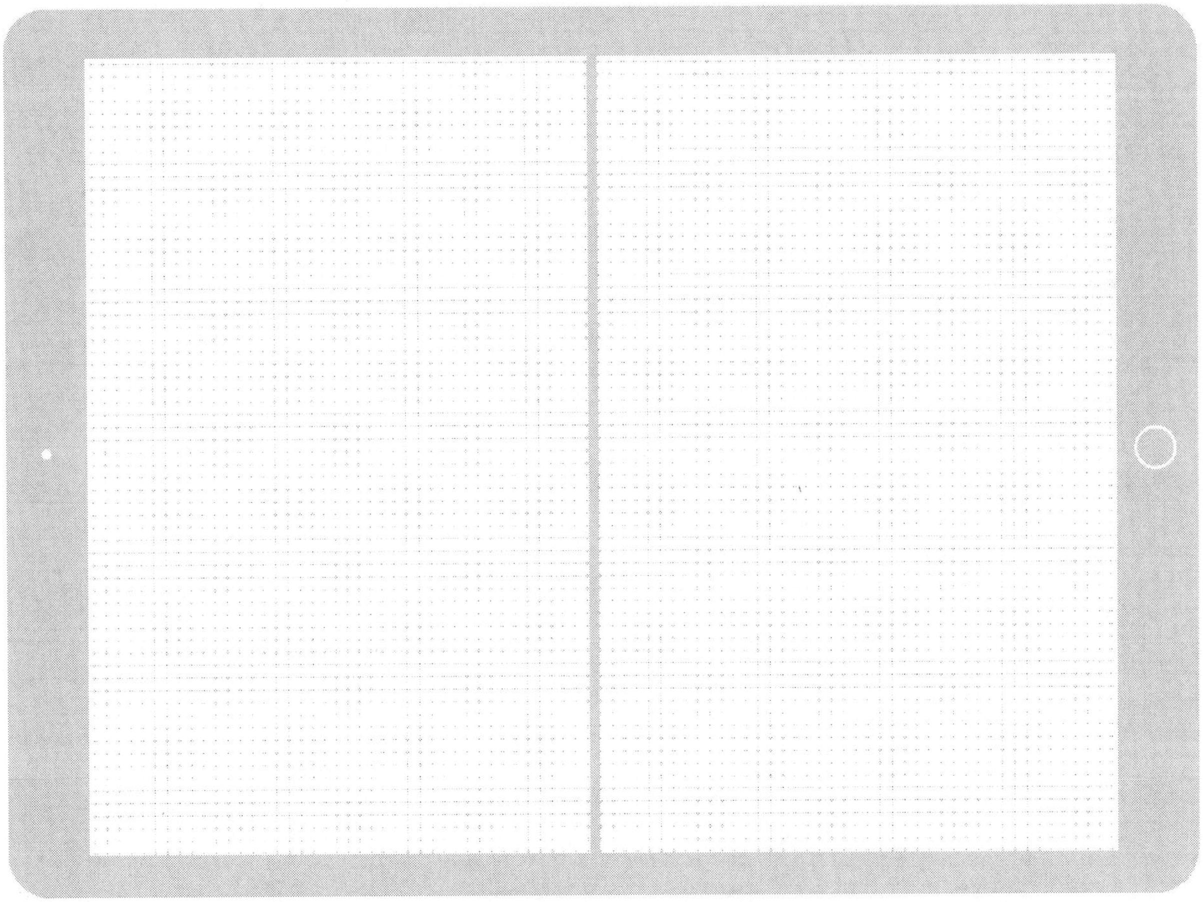

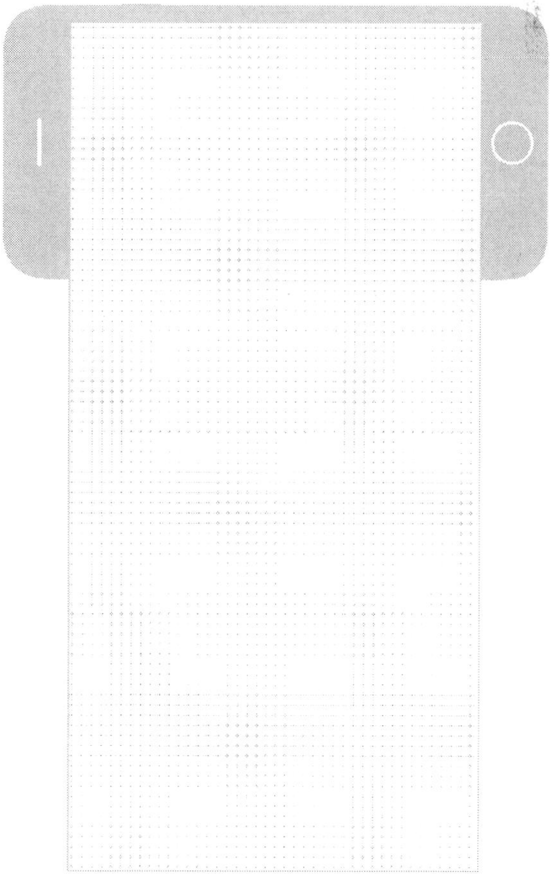

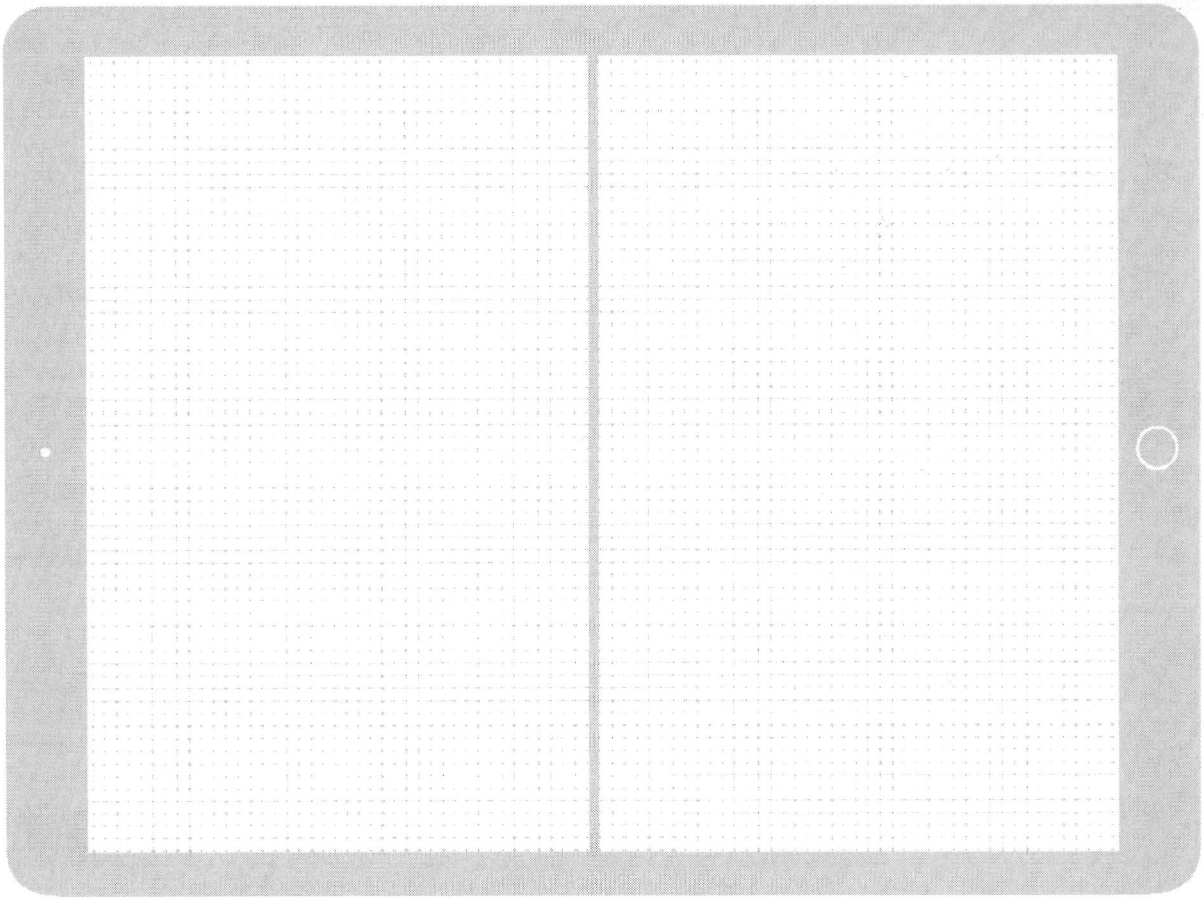

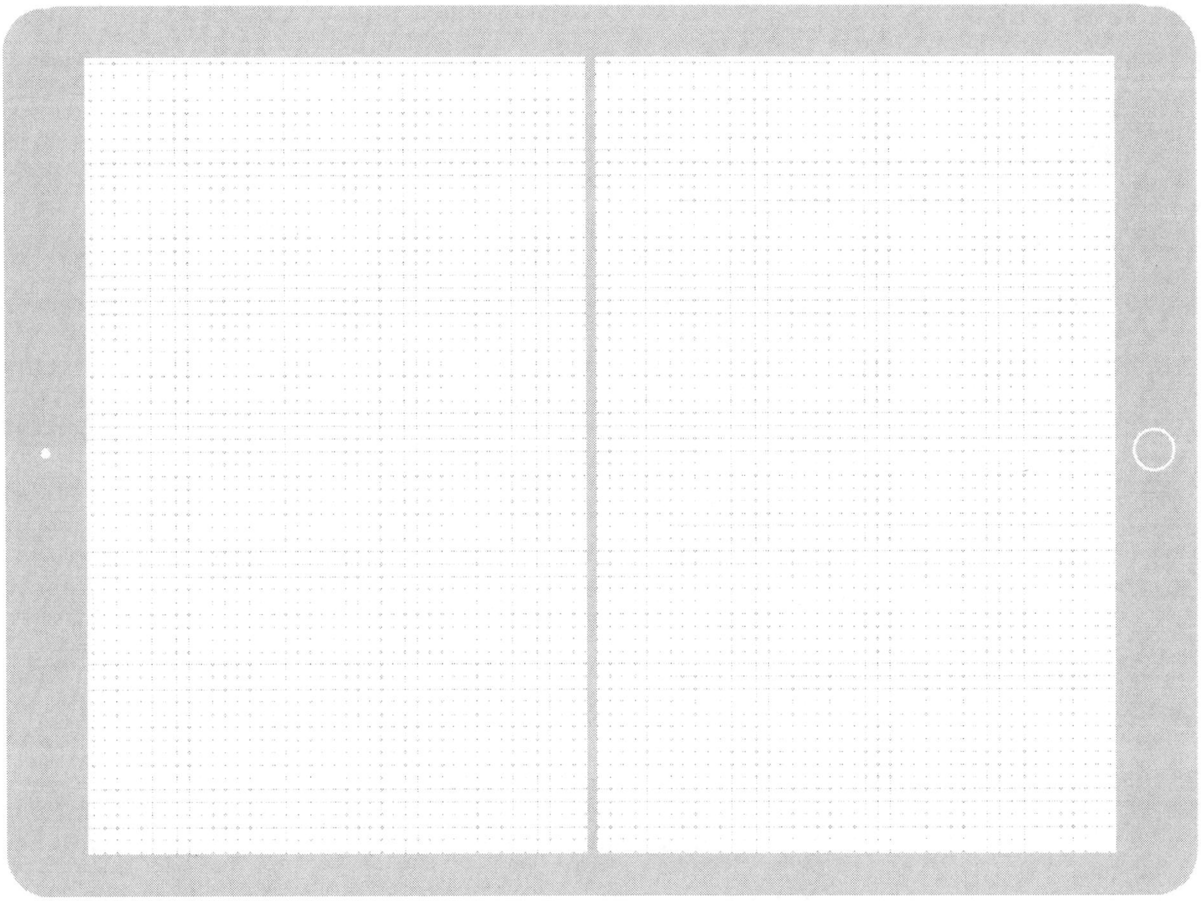

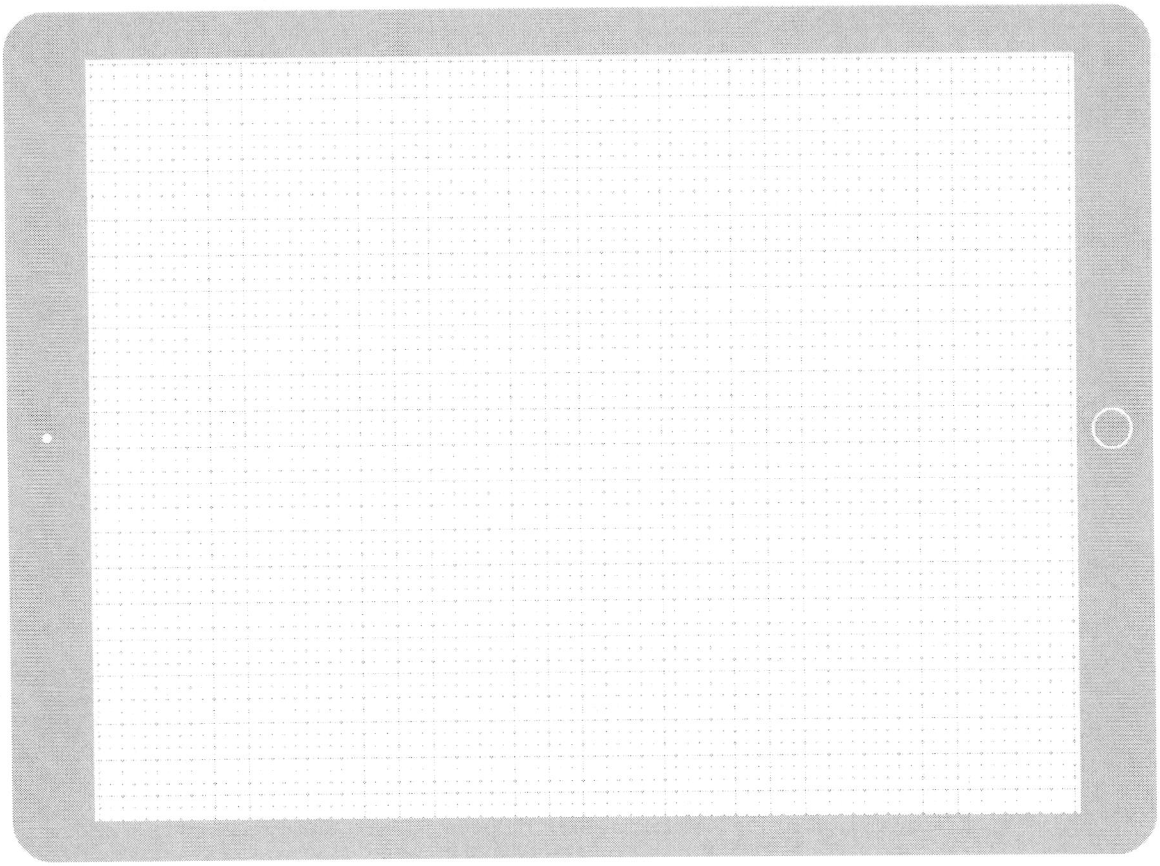

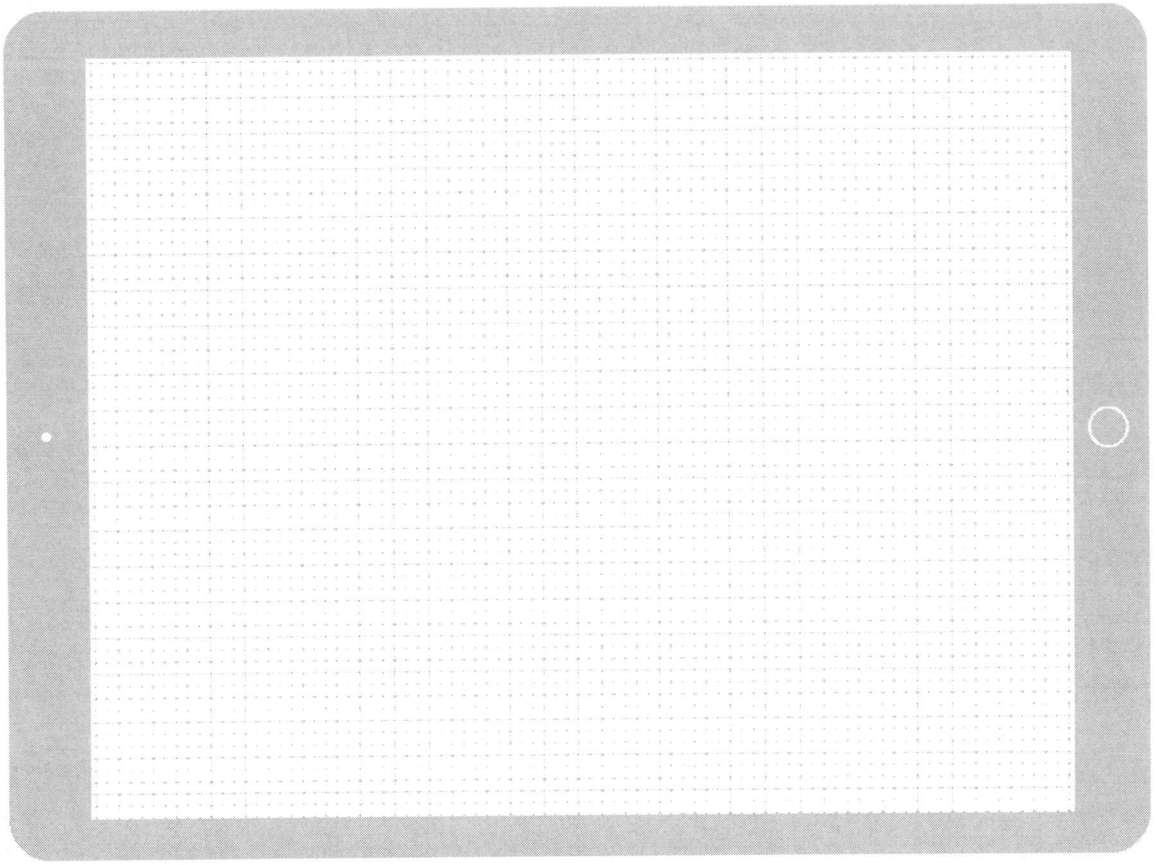

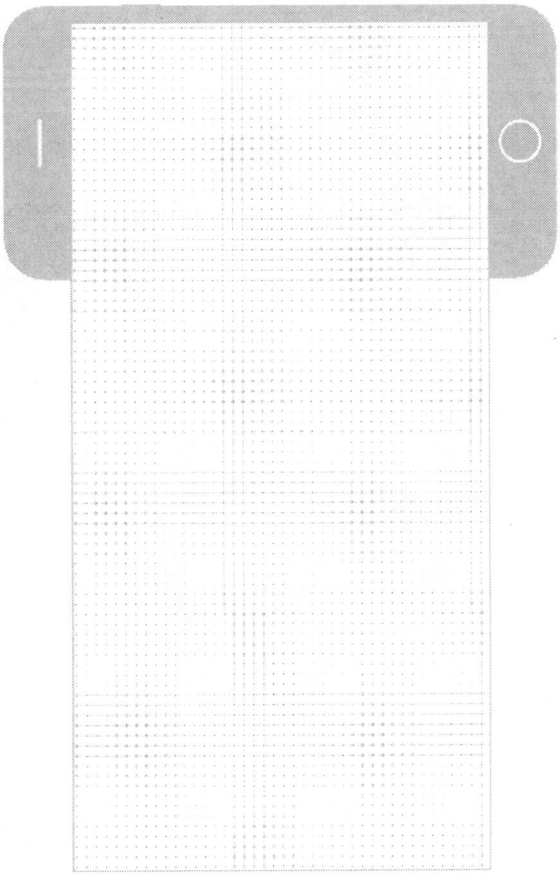

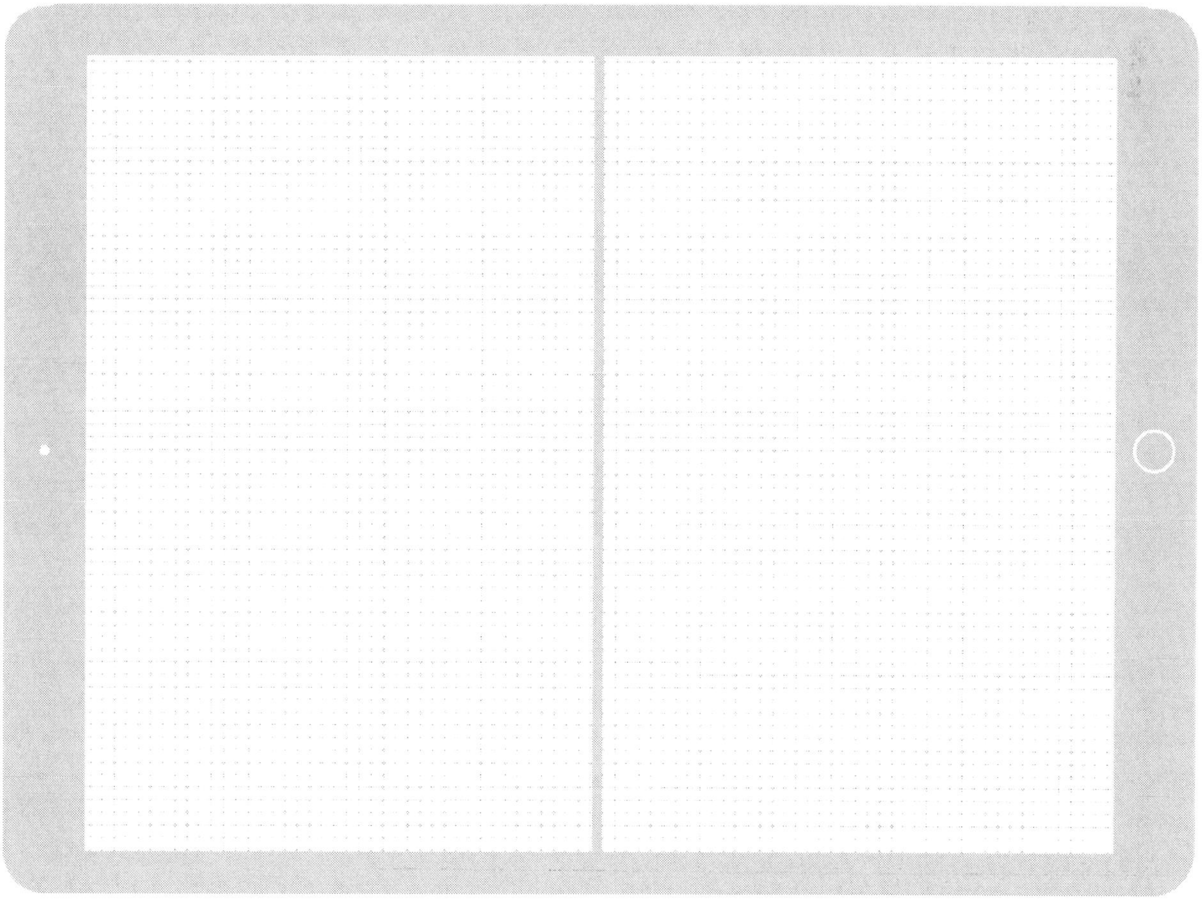

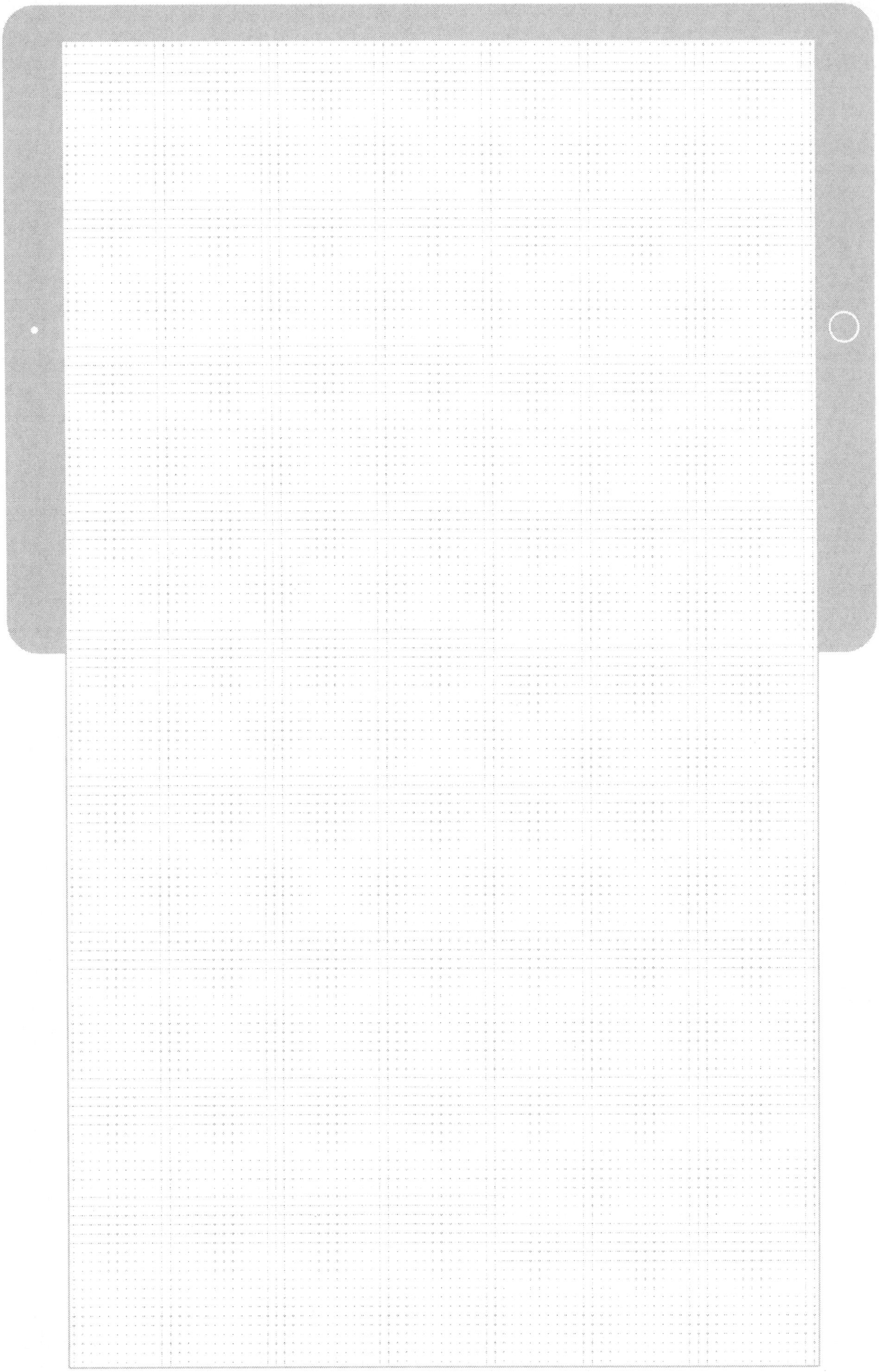

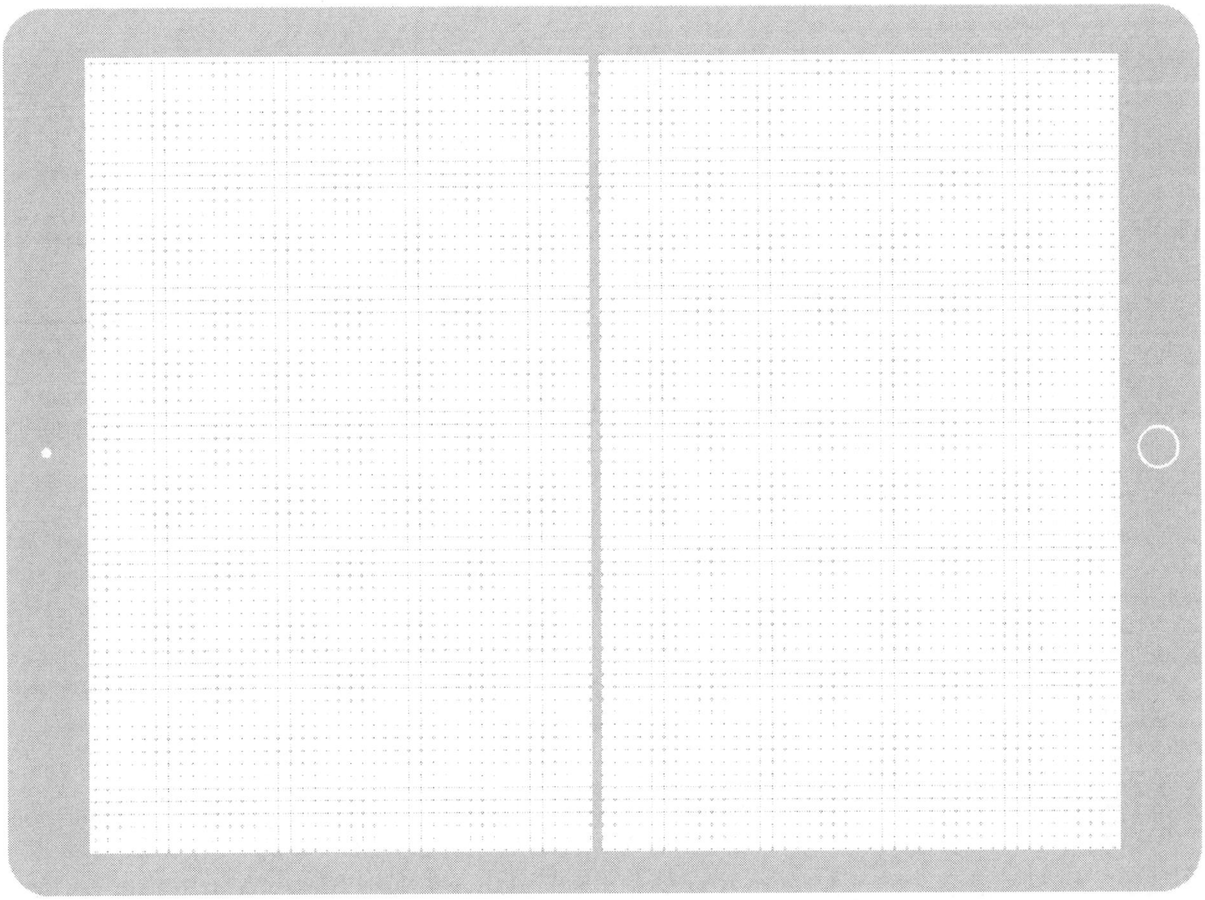

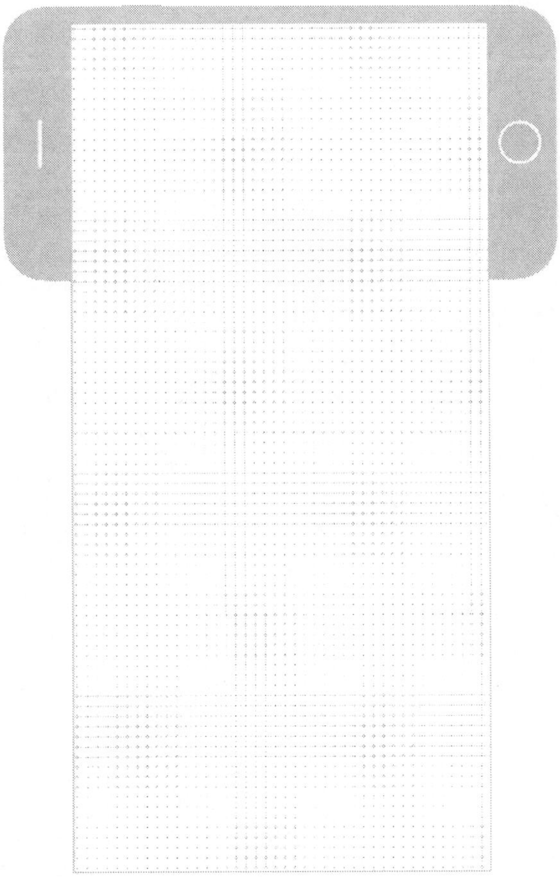

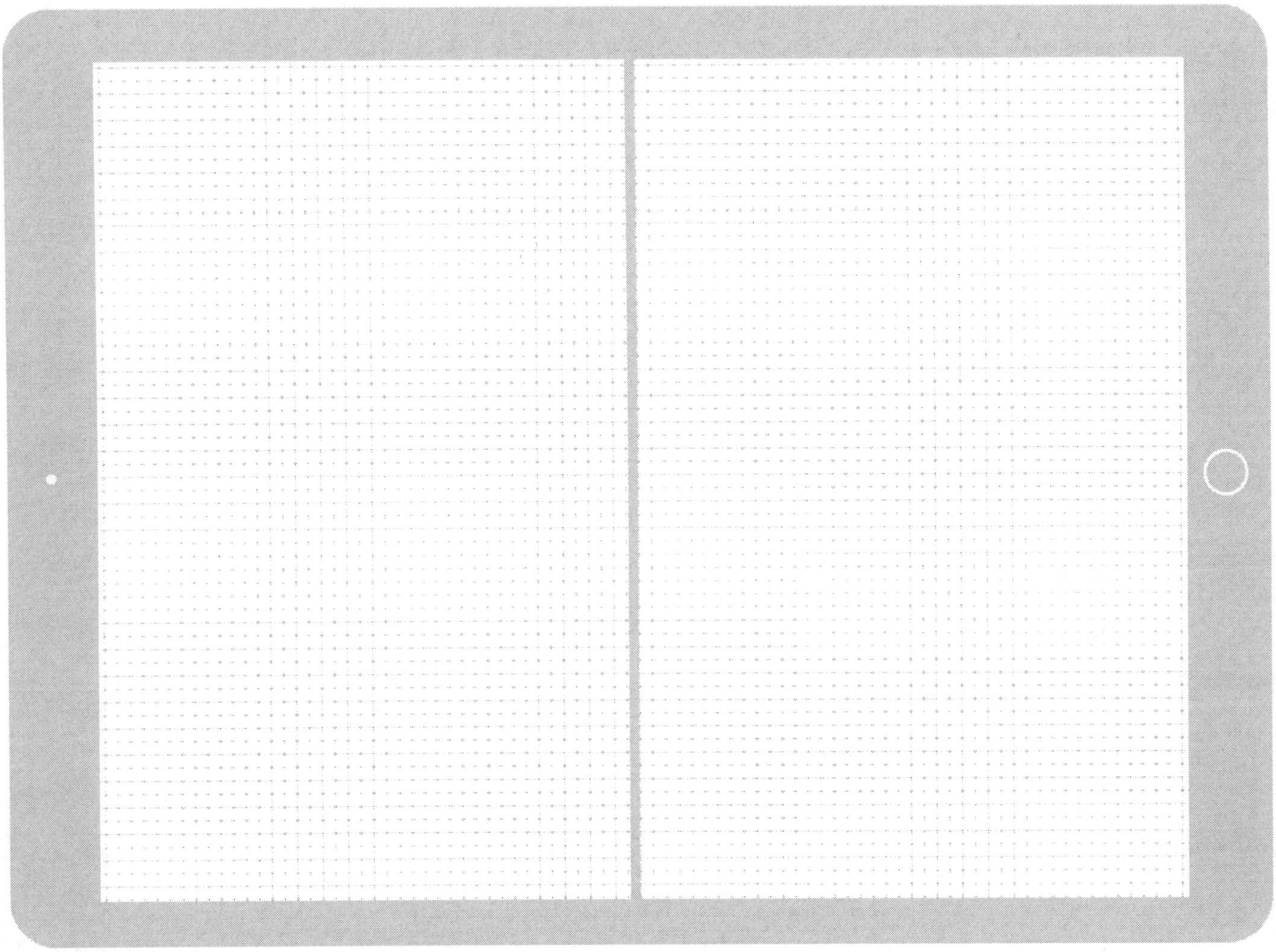

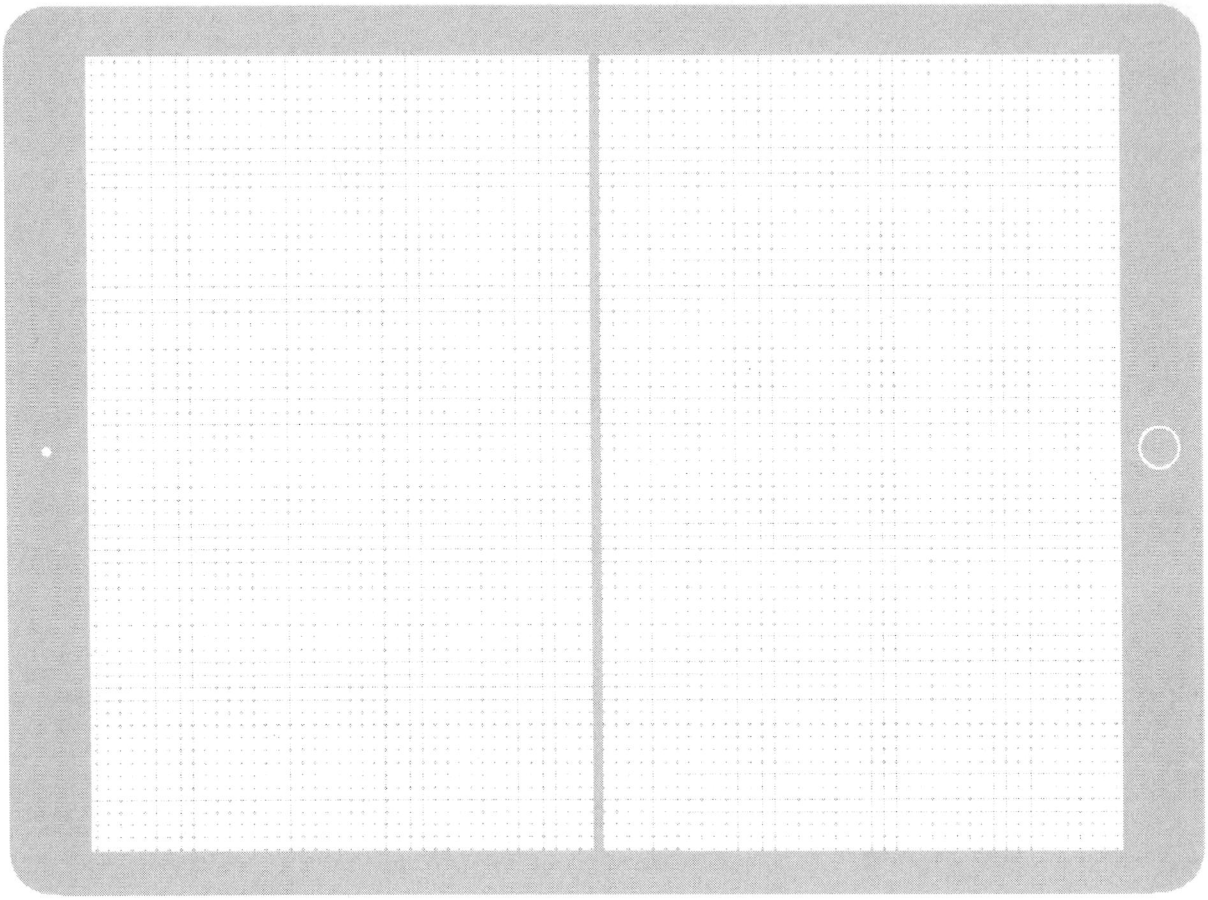

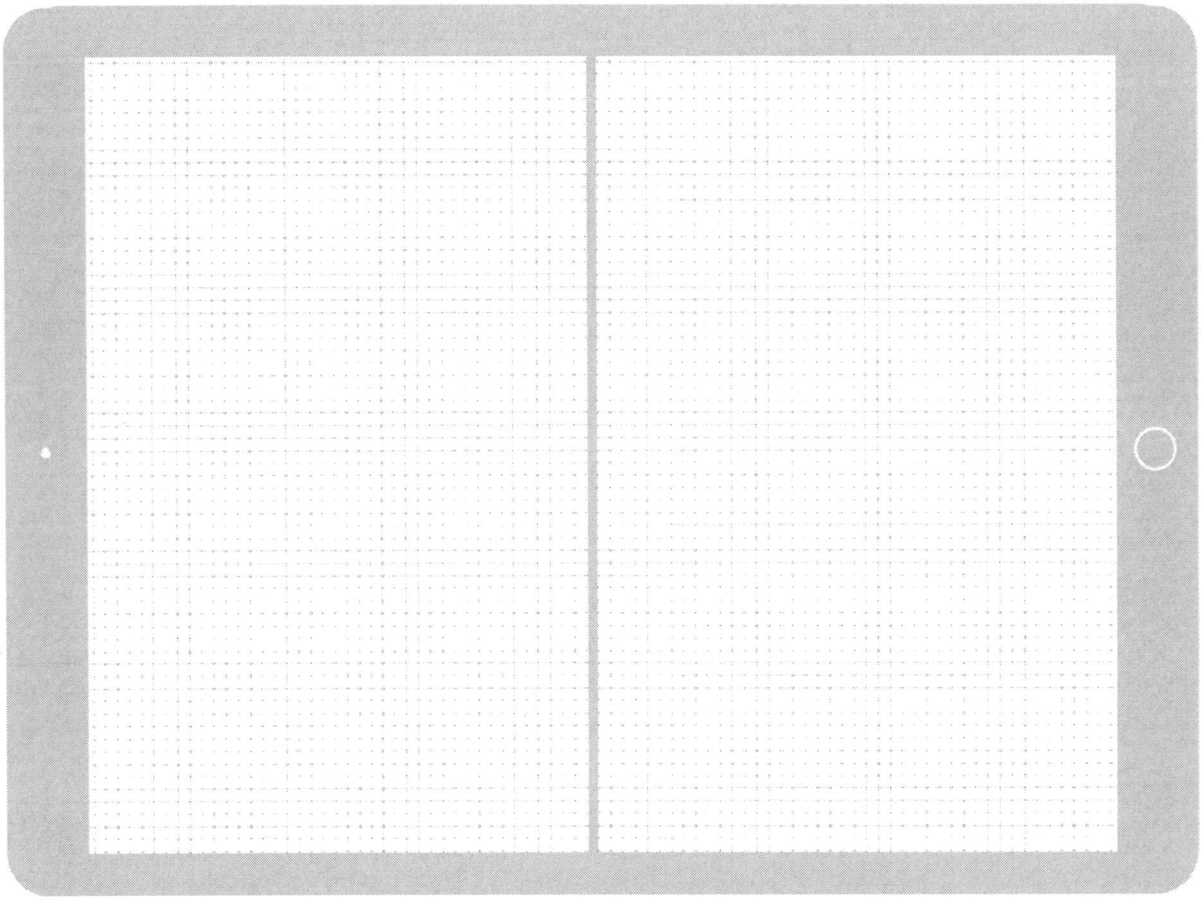

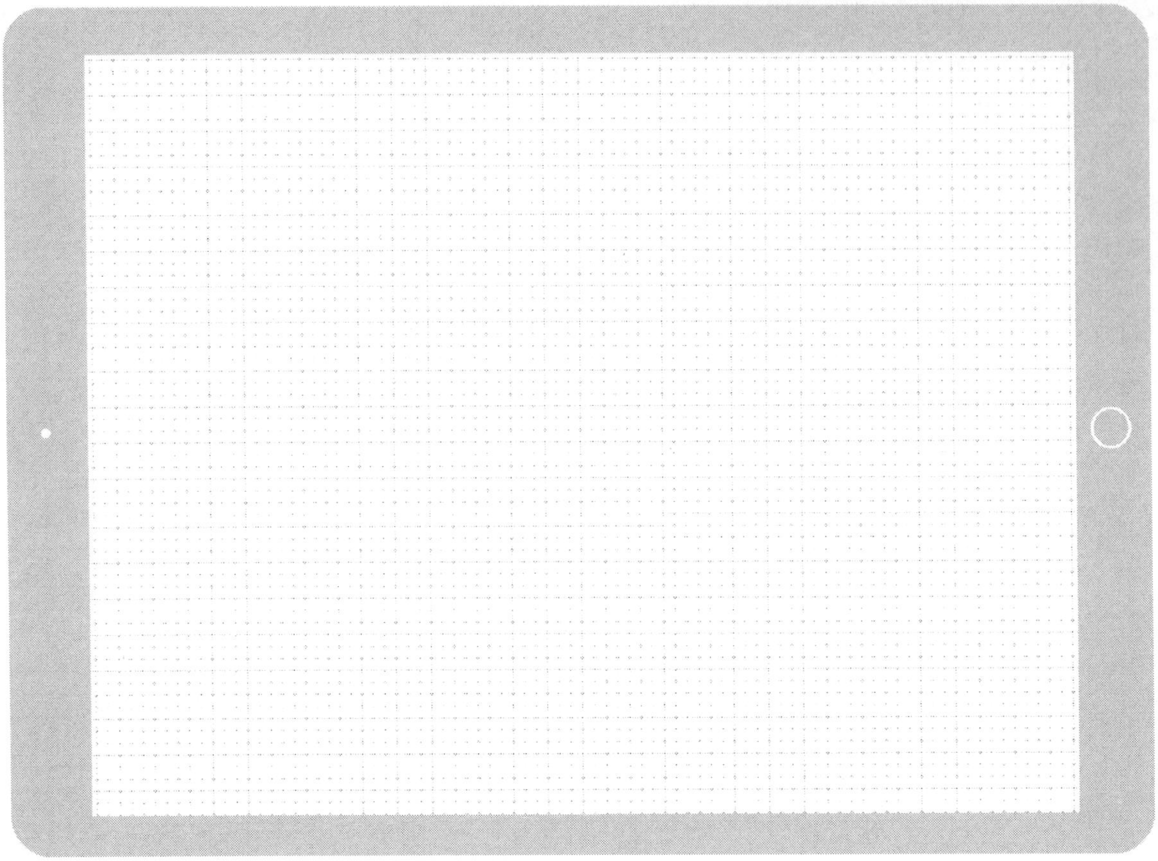

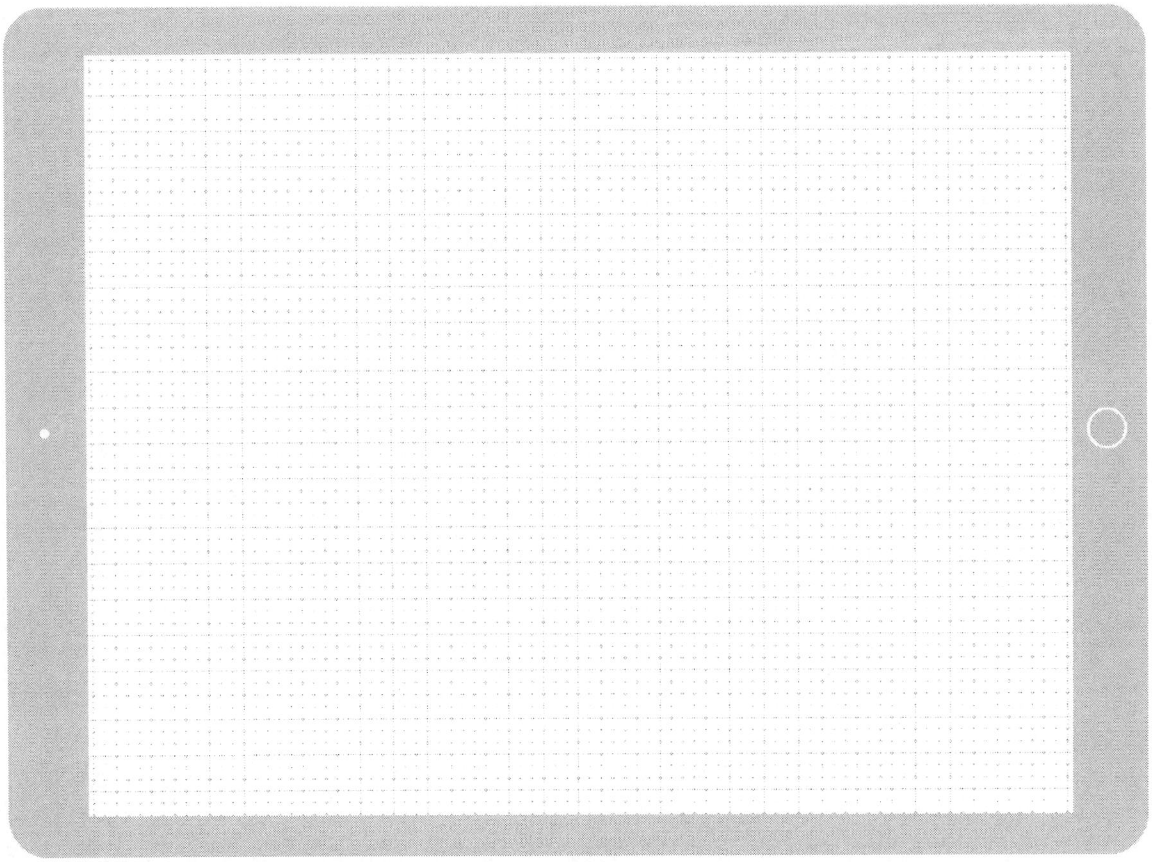

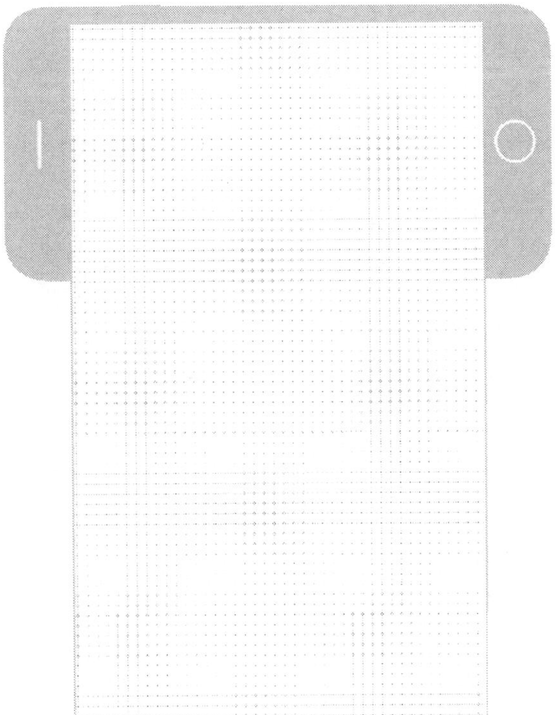

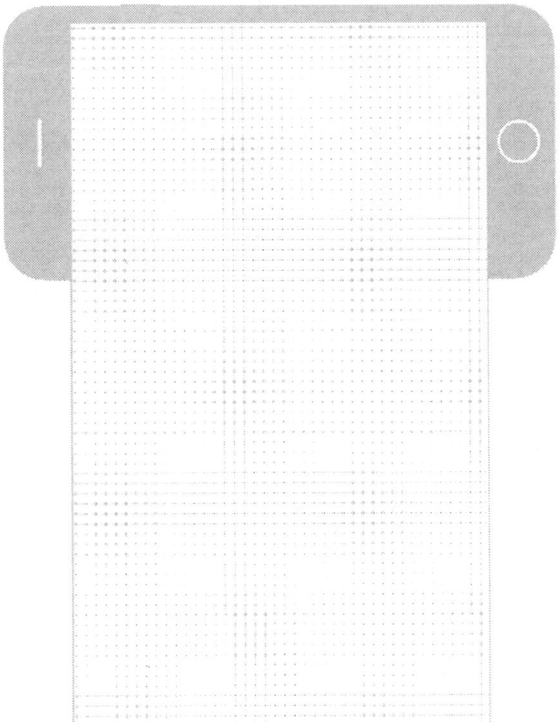

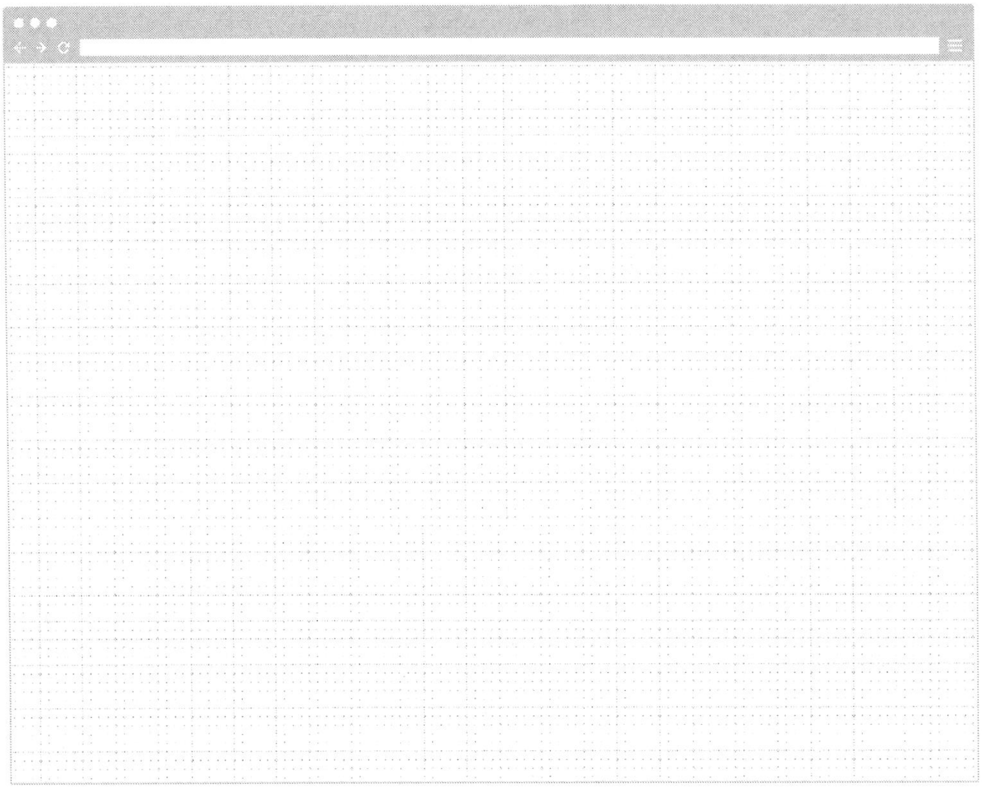

Made in the USA
Columbia, SC
19 August 2022

65685999R00067